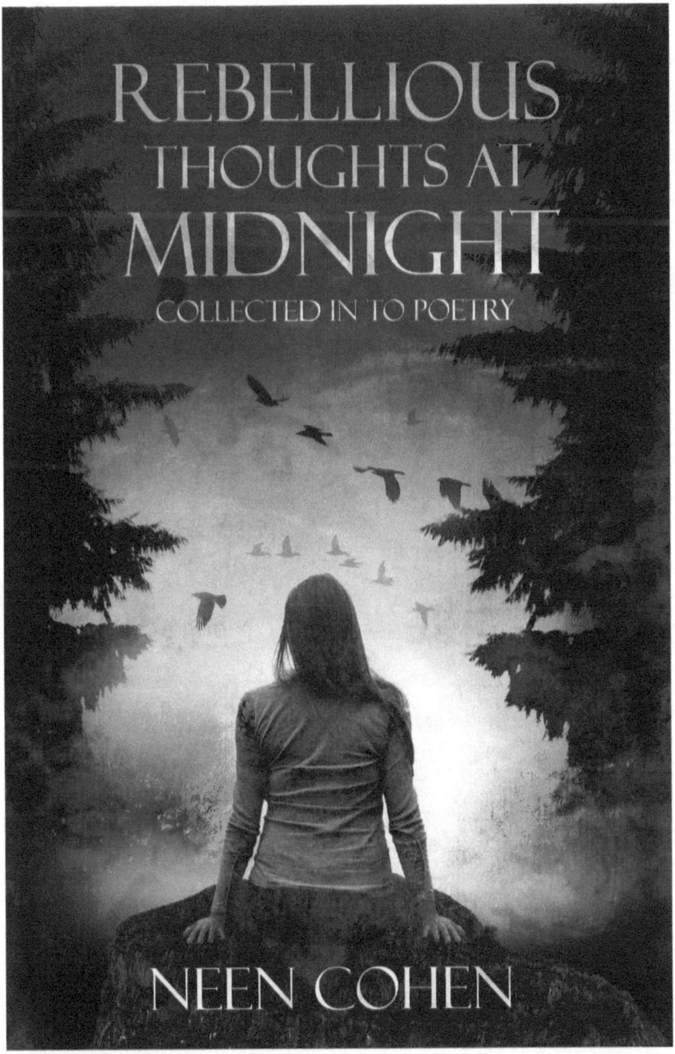
REBELLIOUS
THOUGHTS AT
MIDNIGHT
COLLECTED IN TO POETRY
NEEN COHEN

Copyright © Neen Cohen

All rights reserved.

No part of this publication may be reproduced, distributed, or transmitted in any form or by any means, including photocopying, recording, or other electronic or mechanical methods, without the prior written permission of the publisher, except as permitted by copyright law. For permission requests, contact neen@neencohen.com

Book Cover by Greg Chapman

Preface

Poetry and I go way back. We've been friends, and lovers. Strangers and enemies. Sometimes all at the same moment.

But without a doubt, my relationship with poetry has always been chaotic in nature, to the chagrin of every teacher, lecturer, tutor, and poet enthusiast who handed me a collection they swore would change my life.

Few of them did, but those ones I still adore to this day and hold precious the people who introduced me to the words that healed or opened my life exactly when I needed. The other collections I've mostly used to prop up the always uneven coffee tables of my life.

And now here I am, using this incredible means of short form writing to play with the words I've collected over the years. I've pressed my own midnight chaos in to the pages in the hopes y'all might feel the emotions resonate within yourselves.

Thank you for chancing a change by giving my words a try.

Neen

About the author

Neen Cohen is an Aussie sapphic speculative fiction author. Her novel The Void, won the Page Turner Awards for best LGBT book of 2024. Her foray in to poetry began in 2020 with a co-written collection, Forgiving Reflections. She assumed the poetic side of her had been exorcised. It turned out she was dead wrong.

Neen thrives on being the hyperactive bookworm who rarely stops smiling or laughing, except at midnight when rebellious thoughts tempt her in to insomnia and are sometimes deep, sometimes sweet, and are even sometimes a bit cheeky.

If she ever had to decide between never reading or never writing again she simply wouldn't. Rules were never her strong point.

When not writing or working at the day job, Neen loves nothing more than dancing, nerf wars with the boys, roaming graveyards and forests, playing the PS, and crafting wild and crazy things sometimes for the kiddo and other times simply because she can.

In her ideal world, Neen would spend her days wandering graveyards for inspiration before finding the perfect tree (usually within said graveyard) to lean against and write.

To keep up to date on Neen Cohen's adventures you can find all the links here:

neencohen.com/links

Also by

Novels by Neen Cohen
The Void
Coffee, Cars, and Necromancy
Children of the Gods

Novels with Adrian J Smith
Love Tails and Battle Wails Series
Book 1: Deep Sounding Chaos
Book 2: Surface Pressure
Book 3: Battle Fluke

To my boys who are the biggest planets in my solar system, thank you for staying the course and understanding when I needed to be moving and when I needed to disappear. Thank you for your faith and love in knowing I will always come back to you.

To all those who didn't know I wrote poetry thank you for pointing out the words I hid from the world and giving me the courage to step up and out of the shadows.

For all the insomniacs out there, I hope you find some words to carry in your pocket and help the midnight hour ease you in to dawn.

Contents

Collector	1
Mastering	5
Your Eyes	7
Sunday Afternoon	9
Mirrors	11
Time	13
Irrelevant	15
Why am I not an Ice Queen?	17
Past Secret	19
Sucks to be a Chameleon	21
Sterile and Dirty	23

Politeness	25
For the First Time	27
Baptism	29
I Used to Smile	31
Too Bright	33
Climbing Trees	35
Bubbles	37
Whisky on the Rocks	39
Balconies	41
Complicated Now	43
Fearing Fear	45
She Could have Stumbled	47
Permission to Love	49
Poetic Pain	51
Red Wine	53
Unmedicated	55
How much worse I could have been	57
Raw and Bleeding	59
Rainbows	61
A Box	63

Simple Touch	65
Motherhood	67
Belly Dancer	69
Petrichor	71
Scared and Silent	73
Regrowth	77
Walking Sticks are no light matter	79
Pinwheels	81
100 Years	83
Forbidden Birthday	85
Second or Last	89
Kissed Me	91
Protector	93
Never Lonely Love	95
PTSD	97
Peace	99
Death is not the end	101
Regrets	103
Self Awareness	105
Only Kind of Perfect	107

Beautiful Tears	109
Rebellion	111
A Story of Words	113
Acknowledgements	115
Also by	119
Chapter	124

Collector

I collect words like others might collect stamps
Or something far cooler
I had never been interested in.

I play with the sounds in my mouth
Unsure how to pronounce my treasures
The new words I've stumbled over
And tangle my tongue in the attempt
Not to appear stupid
As stupid as the country girl
They once branded me to be

Through collecting and finding
Digging and searching
I found new definitions and meanings
That don't make me feel small

Words shouldn't be used to trap
But to unlock the cages
The ones they shoved me in to
Kicking and screaming
Until I had nothing left

I collect words like pebbles
And give them eagerly, willingly
To those who can find beauty in the shadows
And strength in the darkness

I collect them for myself
And turn them into shining stones
and sparks of light

 I throw them up with joy and watch
As the glitter of my words
Brush against tear stained faces and
Turn sobs in to laughter

I collect words to be seen
And to show others that they were never invisible
I can be gentle and kind
And maybe when they are finished
with my offered pebbles and glitter

They tuck a few into their own pocket
Collecting them as their own
As they move on

And prepare to share the collections
of their own recollections.

Mastering

It's a horrible thought, this one of mastering
That even still weighs me down in the darkened hours

I lift my phone, groaning
As I work out the remaining potential of sleep
It diminishes each time I roll over
And give in to the temptation to lift the device again

To master anything in this life
Fills me with an ice cold horror
As though something deadly
Were pushed into my veins
Beneath the uncomfortable
Itching tape they have stuck
To my bruised and heavy elbow

I don't aim to master, I never wanted it
They repeated the need over and over
And I relive it all, some 20 years later
In those endless hours of sleeplessness

I still don't want to become the best of anything
That is one of many hells I fight against

Perfectionism was heralded as close to God
But why should I have ever cared
about someone I'd never met

I'd drag my feet behind their steps
And wonder if I would ever wake from the nightmare
But it was all a trick, and I the fool
I was the tick in the column of different.

Maybe mastering that would've gotten them
Off my back and let me explore the world
My way, without perfection and mastering
Without the red bloody ink of damning ticks
But with a smiley face sticker in the
Column of difference

Your Eyes

Shirt hems pulled out of shape
Twisted in nervous fingers
That never stop moving
Scratching, tearing, ripping

Keep moving
Keep moving
Don't stop
Don't let them see

The shake in your movements
The hesitation in your voice
Let your hair frame your face
Hide behind the strands

And cover the blush of your cheeks
But above all
Hide your eyes

Sunday Afternoon

The small of my back aches
from leaning over the table.
Even as a child,
Sunday routines were well established

I quickly despised the dresses
and the morning droning voices
of old white men who told me all the things
I could be and the things I could do,
that would send me to hell.

But the afternoons were mine.

I rub my hand over the small of my back
leaning into the touch and hearing the feint pop

A sigh escapes my lips
Squeezing my eyes tight

I blink away the small details of my task
and look again
at the picture on the puzzle box

The smell of wood and the brightness of repetitive colours
bring back Sunday afternoons, when I can breathe
no longer letting Sunday mornings hold a knife to my chest

Mirrors

They say beauty is in the eye of the beholder
Well shit, no wonder I've always hated mirrors

Time

Time was a cruel mistress.
It was used as a weapon;
it's ticking down,
there's always tomorrow,
but it's been so long.

Until we are finally told
The future isn't promised
The past is where it belongs

And the things that do not serve you
Do not have to hold you

It's a choice
Just like forgiveness

Irrelevant

They roll their eyes
as I stop once again, crouching down
to watch the small animal
making the giant trek over the furry leaf
I stand, a smile on my face
Scanning the trees and shrubs around me

I am on my own giant leaf.
Or maybe I am the head lice
On the giant who stomps and shakes the earth
Beneath their shoes and my bare feet.
The giant who showers until we are washed away.

The words bubble out of me
Effervescence in a glass they would shatter
With their aggressive clinks.

They don't smile at my imaginings
They furrow their brows
And ask me how God would feel about this,
About my nonsense

But it's not a question I can answer
Even if they had given me time enough.

Because I had no idea.
Did God think like me or like them?

That's when I learnt that my answers
were entirely irrelevant.

Why am I not an Ice Queen?

Questions ring in my head like gongs calling all to attention.
Why do I keep letting myself get hurt?
The onus on myself
And the responsibility removed from
The abusers
The users
The liars
And the thieves
I ask myself over and over

like a mantra
Why do you keep letting yourself get hurt?

Those who have been given so much
Of my flesh and bone, my thoughts
And wild brave imaginings.
Bruise and batter me with side eyes
And mocking laughs
They tease and joke
And I'm always the butt at the end
Why am I such a slow learner?

I open up to the connections
And trust my tendered flesh to their administrations
That feel gentle until they aren't
Until they get tired and bored
Sick of the gentle ways I yearn

to be touched, to be treated, to be loved
Why am I not an ice queen yet?

Past Secret

I know now that
past Neen was a shell
She never saw anything about herself worth while
even the interesting dramas in her life were all
her siblings' or extended family's
she was nothing until
this girl made her something
even if that something was nothing but a secret,
at least Past Neen was a fun secret
Until she wasn't

Sucks to be a Chameleon

You can't please everyone all the time
But this chameleon sure has tried
No matter how many times
She reads, or hears, or tries
to convince herself
That this is her motto
That pleasing others is all in vain
She still cares too much about the mysterious 'them'

The stranger down the road
who scowled at her
And the person who judged
The only thing she thought she had to offer

The chameleon fears
The power to change will one day end
And she will remain stuck

In the limbo space
Of nothing

Sterile and Dirty

Sterile conversations and memories
Emotions washed away and
Washed clean in the toxic air

Heartbeats that don't exist here
Because it's just another alien planet
Hostile and uninhabitable
Until you close your eyes
Until you let down your guard

In a moment of laughter and fun
Dirty bath water slams you into the ground
Your hand reaches behind, automatically
It presses on the part that moves when it shouldn't
Another sharp knife's point digging and twisting

Politeness

Politeness was an unnatural
Distaste on my tongue
Like ashes and wax
Strangers
Siblings
Judgements and offence
Bad health cures it all
Death the eternal peacemaker

For the First Time

She tastes like bourbon and coke
Smelling like an absent father figure
Her lips are softer than flower petals
Even when she laughs about other conquests.

We share a history
And very little interests.

But her fingers only need graze my skin
And nothing else matters.
Age, history, interests
Float away on the drunken air
Fading away as I feel beautiful
For the first time

Baptism

Don't.
Stop.
Never.
Wrong.

Lists of what not to do
Were the words I was baptised in

They washed over me as I cursed and slashed
Seering through the anger
And the self hatred

Tasting salt on my lips
and on my hands

I Used to Smile

She never understood
How I could be alone and happy
She never understood the pleasures
I took in being within my own thoughts

So she lashed out
With words as swords
Made wrong something that
Always gave me joy,
calm and peace

I let her take that power from me
Until I hated being alone
In my own thoughts

Water and solitude sprang tears and anger
Every single time

In the mirror was a face
I didn't know
A face
I hated
The face I missed
hidden
Somewhere beneath
unreachable

Until one day
I saw the sea of yellow faces
Following the sun across the sky

And I remembered how much I used to smile

Too Bright

I am a me shaped shadow marring the landscape
With the shape I'm not.
Making blurring the shape they thought I should be
A corner,
a corner,
a corner!
It's all I ever wanted

With my back pressed against connecting walls
The shade and shadow keeping me safe

But a spotlight is what I got

Climbing Trees

I miss climbing trees
The confidence I once had in my body; gone
The abilities; broken
I left them on the floor
Next to that wall
It and my shoulder too well acquainted
Bruised and battered
Was I not Deserving?

Never an apology
Never an excuse

I left them unspoken there
And one day
I will dream about climbing trees again

Bubbles

He called me bubbles

And he wasn't wrong

I lived the life of bubbles

Disconnected

And praised

For my precarious happiness

Whisky on the Rocks

A golden waterfall flows over the frozen blocks
Warped in patterned crystal
It burns as it goes down,
A pleasurable pain

She drinks like a man
And she's heard it all her life

She throws back the last of the liquid
Chewing on a half melted sliver of ice

She rattles the rest against the glass
She'll have another one

Balconies

The important things happened on balconies
With views of distance cities
That were never my own

Thoughts flowed
Uncrowded by solid walls

Her strength held me
Like the cement beneath us
Words I never thought
Tumbled from my mouth

In that moment
I cursed the freedom
And blamed my own lack of guard
To the balcony and the darkness

Things were never the same
But the confession made us stronger
Connected on levels
We had only ever feared for each other

Complicated Now

When did it all get so complicated

The earth, and the trees
They used to be enough

Fresh air was precious
And fire was respected

Green meant something different
And the world was a magical ball
To discover

Fearing Fear

She looks at me with interest
And intrigue
With wonder and a little fear
And in her eyes I imagine I can see
the cage with the sticks to poke
At the contradictions
Ones I've hated forever
Unable to settle on one thing
That I am
That I am not
She speaks of fear and a
Get out of jail free card
But perhaps it's the reality of people
Who refuse to make up their mind
And limit their time here

Or maybe it is as simple as fear

She Could have Stumbled

Flames or smoulders are the only choice
For those who know too early
who they are

They rise fast and burning
A blazing star of beauty
Doomed and betrayed by certainty

They leave the rest of us behind
In the cold and the dark

And I wade through too many years
Of uncertainty and fear

But she burned too fast and too bright
And how I wish she had only stumbled
Just a few times, so she could be here now
Instead of in the halls of Valhalla

Permission to Love

Connection and acceptance
Were fake and forged
Under pretenses
Under layers and lies
Silence was the worse kind
Making guessing games
At pinpointing the problems
Taking years longer then needed

I heard that gravelly voice
That passion and desire
Permission to be allowed

to be ourselves

Forging the way through
Bigotry and hate
Finding light and Love
And self-acceptance

Poetic Pain

Head has started pounding again
Taken the last pills
Coffee is brewing

... is t his poetic enough

For who?

Red Wine

I've spilt too many secrets
and confessed my soul's desires,
on red wine.

I should know better by now!

Unmedicated

Admiration and inspiration
Two coins and both as deadly
If reality is warped
And you can't see the mirror

The past and the truth
Holding yourself to
Imaginary standards

Seeing someone else's end scene
When you are still in your first act

Judgements are unhealthy
And races aren't being run

Stop and breath
See the mirror

Find the smile
The peace
The beauty
The love

Exhaustion pulls the last scratched words
From the spilling ink
Tomorrow.

Tomorrow we will talk to the doctor
Tomorrow we will let them see

But finally
Sleep stops the trains running into each other

How much worse I could have been

'So It's about control'
She says it as though
I haven't realised, known, ruminated
On my need, and my lack of it
Over a lifetime of self examination
and Criticisms

'Hmmm it comes back to control'
Her eyebrows lift as if I hadn't known this before,
and during, and after
Every single thing I chose to do
That I 'shouldn't' have
According to *their* rules

Was any of it more than a middle finger in the air
as I quietly fought for some control
Of my own life?

I reexamine and ask the questions
that make me shift in my seat
Make me feel this discomfort
that I'm supposed to lean in to

And I think of all the things I never tried that were listed
Alongside the (mis)adventurous paths
I skipped down

Oh how much worse I could have been
How much more I could have done
to give them more fodder
For their Sunday Afternoon gossip sessions
disguised as charity for the wayward sisters

Raw and Bleeding

Words were turned into arrows
aimed and loosed
to tear through my flesh

Fear threatens to expel
The contents of my stomach
As I see what remains of me
Left in the desert of self loathing

Organs and muscles pulse in chaotic patterns
While dark arterial blood oozes and spurts from holes
left behind where the wind stings with its caress
of the torn open skin and hanging sinew

They hiss through their teeth and gasp to stifle their screams

as they protect the innocent from the sight of my carcass
while it's picked apart and fought over by the vultures
who
waited and watched while the poison tipped words
pierced my body over and over again

Rainbows

She learned to love rainbows
Through healing bruises

A Box

Within a box within a box
Hidden and unacknowledged

They forget about your existence

My anger burns
I fear it will destroy you
Destroy your calm balance
Your equilibrium with being invisible

But you shouldn't have to hide
The pain and the loneliness

I will fight for Your light
For the boxes to open

For the sun to see
You and your brilliance

Simple Touch

She reminds me of a strength
I'm not sure I ever had

But I lift my head and smile
The energy swirls around me

And I feel small fingers push into mine

Motherhood

A stone, heavy
Like the one strapped to Atlas
Presses against me
Pins me to my anxiety and fear

I smell his hair and cup his face
His laugh, always but a breath away

I will condemn the whole world
To keep him safe

Belly Dancer

Dancing flames are a sweet salvation
The heat rises and you feel alive
Images of risking more and getting closer

It's seduction moving in the rhythm
Of hips and fire

Kissing and blistering your
brow and flesh
Each shadow whispers
Secrets and desires

It should know better
Then to tease you like a belly dancer

Petrichor

They have a name for my love
Of the rain hitting the ground
The green feeling that washes around me
Washes away that tight fist in my chest
And the ache in my back

They have a name for my love
Of self isolation and solitude
Those moments when only my core
Essence matters or exists

Thoughts and emotions washing past me
In a river of unconcern

They have a name for my love
Of rough bark between palm and sole

Pressed and biting
Feeling alive and connected to something
So much bigger than myself

They have a name for my love

Scared and Silent

She was scared and silent
Too silent
Until she wasn't
And when she wasn't
they Tut tutted
At her booming voice and her sneer

So she stepped back
Scared and silent and angry

Too angry

They hissed and scowled
Until she stopped caring
And when she stopped caring
They fawned over her

Prayed and cursed in the same language
The same words

So she stepped back
Scared and silent and angry and caring

Too caring

Too emotional and hysterical
Those harsh scoldings
with eyes and lips

Until she wasn't

Until she was nothing but a shell
That they picked apart
Telling each other about the days when

 She was scared and silent and angry and caring

So they blame the now
But the now sees the sun and the smiles

The now never scolds or tuts
The now allows her to bloom
And she doesn't have to worry
About being

Permission is never required for her to be

Scared or silent or angry or caring
She's loved for being all of them

Regrowth

Her wings had been stolen
Ripped and torn off
Pain inflicted upon her with each plucked feather

She sobbed, in a foetal position
for several lifetimes
Until the thirst itched at her throat

On trembling legs she walked,
feeling a new sting in her shoulder blades
Reaching back she felt the gentle swell
Of newformed buds waiting to open

She smiled as she walked, the tremble disappearing
Enjoying the feel of the dirt on her bare soles

The novelty made her find beauty again
Now that pain had its expiry date

Walking Sticks are no light matter

Her laugh echoed around the hills
and bounced off the trees
sending unseen critters
skittering to her joyous
and rambunctious volume

'Oh that's a perfect one.'
she pipes up before I realise anyone sees
As I test the large branch
that had lain abandoned on the track

'It's too big for her.' His voice taunts
But she doesn't even acknowledge him

Instead she asks to look at it
and with her expert eye she weighs
and tests and hmms and haaas

Before she hands it back with a smile that
sparkles alive in her eyes
'It's a perfect find.'

Pinwheels

Spinning wheels of colour
Turned by the sun
Have such little control
And power over their own beauty

The patterns that light up eyes
And small smiles are not dictated
By the pinwheels actions
But how it chooses to react

They are simply a beautiful means
To show what otherwise
Would pass us by
Unseen and too often unfelt

But the pinwheel moves
While staying in place
Finding beauty where others might
Thrash against being still

It will not let the limitations
Convince it to believe in it's stillness
Because it moves how it can
To become it's most beautiful

100 Years

I scratch more names into the paper

Sometimes the pages are lined
keeping me in check
But today, my writing slants on its own
Angling my inspirations
As thoughts tumble around

Making immortal those that have no one left
To visit or chat to them
To keep them appraised
of the progress or set backs
Of this world
that continues to turn, nourished
with their forgotten blood and bones.

My legs tingle beneath me
I have sat for too long
Fingers tracing a name
That might have been Herbert or Harold
So little remains in the depressions of the stone

I yearn for the tools of
Dinosaur bone hunters
to brush away
The tiny fragments
And perhaps reveal the truth
Behind the person who died
Over a hundred years ago.

Forbidden Birthday

Over the years she taught me to splatter paint
and admire the little scribbles
Of imperfect ink made of lines and dashes
In a creatives morse code

Hurried hands scrunch my paper
In fists that still my heart as they clean
and tidy before popping to the shops
for a quick minute, 'if that's okay?'
neither of us mind.

The door closes and the engine starts
but I'm already watching as she rescues
my latest attempt at drawing from the walls

She traces the beauty of every crease and
shows me the journey the ink has made

'There's enough time.' She says conspiratorially
But I've given up hope anyone remembers what today is

The yahoo calls from the front of the house
And I'm left to find something to occupy me
In the corner I'm forgotten by them all
as she reads the cards for strangers
the ones she's designed
with her own hands and heart

When they leave there is still enough time
for her to wink at me and pull me in to her side.
She lowers her voice with instruction
and we head out the back where we
close our eyes and listen to the conversation
between the trees

She slips the present in to my hand
and pecks a kiss on my check
'Happy Birthday, my little triplet.'

The twins get home, her actual children
who went out and explored the world
of ice and music with their father

REBELLIOUS THOUGHTS AT MIDNIGHT

I wouldn't have traded places with them
not for all the world.
My day had been filled with magic
and a new deck of cards
I'll tuck into my socks when I get home

Second or Last

Second or last
I learn too slow that they have the same meaning

What they mean is not first
What they mean is
letting someone else drive

Taking a back seat in your own vehicle
It takes someone to say no

Someone who demands you
Hold the wheel to your own life

And never makes you feel
Second, or Last

Kissed Me

When my lips
were cracked and sore.
Dried out from the wind
that tangled my hair into knots
and cooled the sweat on my skin.

We walked along the forest path
Overgrown with wild grass
And filled with dead leaves.

They crunched beneath our feet and
scattered the unseen critters
Deeper into the foliage.

The beauty made me cry
And I smiled self deprecatingly

trying to laugh away
The dynamics no one ever gets

My lips cracked more and I hissed in pain
But she held my face in gentle palms
And kissed me anyway

Protector

Her warm fur presses hard against my leg
She pushes against my steps
And looks up at me with those eyes
That beg not for food
But for her human to stay
To go back to where it's safe

I reach one hand down
And scritch her between her ears
The muscles ripple beneath
Her coat and she wants to enjoy
The touch of her human
But the danger remains

The pressure against my legs
Increases the closer I get
To the front door.

"It's okay, it's just the mailman."
I croon as I look up
And smile through security mesh

"She's a good protector."
He nods approval and I smile with
Honesty and love looking down
With fingers still buried in her fur
And agree to the strangers assessment

He hands me the packages
As we exchange nothing words
she remains at my side
My protector, with her love
And her desire to protect me
From the potential danger
Of every other human

Because she knows that
Just's don't exclude anyone
From becoming a danger.

Never Lonely Love

There's never a lonely moment
Once an animal has bonded themselves
To you and your heart

Mine supervise bathroom visits,
Long baths, and dancing in the kitchen
They ensure I haven't forgotten them
As I hyper-fixate on the next
Story, character, puzzle, show

When as still as I can be
I'm never alone for long
Before one carefully makes their way
To my side, collapsing against my skin
Which vibrates moments later
As their pleasure floods their lithe bodies

And transfers their calmness
In to my own existence.

I need a pocket never-lonely-love
To take with me on those days
When loneliness isn't the calmness
I am searching for

When I am surrounded by people
And what I really need is that space
To take a deep breath and remember
That love comes in many forms and
When I get home
The never lonely love will be there.

PTSD

It was always spoken of
In hushed whispers
About those that had fought
And come back 'not right'

Or about the survivors
Who escaped the brutal fists
Of the ones who should have
Healed and not hurt them

It was a comment so easily spoken
A wave of a hand through the screen
And I always the last to know

In that moment my world tipped
And I leaned. I watched the camera

Capture my ahuh moment
In slow painful misery

PTSD isn't always about the bruises you can show
About the broken bones
And the reports and scans

I never knew religious trauma
Was actually a thing

It was the thing I always joked about
With myself as the punch line

Peace

I try to harness the peace I feel when wrapped
In sunshine and greenery
When the world stops
and time is an invention of strict rules
I struggle to follow on the best of days

And today is not one of those

Today I grasp at peace that lingers out of reach
Away from my fingers
as the darkness of intrusive thoughts
Overwhelms me while I keep the smile in place

For her comfort, and for his
For them and them and them
And each time I do a little more of my true peace

Is chipped away like the edges of crockery
cleaned in modern ways they were never designed for

But the imperfections will not break me or trap me
Into fretting and covering up for their comfort

Not any more

Peace is as much a construction
As time and perfection
And none of these will be my master any longer

I will find peace in my own choosing
In ignoring
In screaming
In laughing and lion breathing

I'll find my peace in not being still
While I'm rocking that boat
Designed for others and their delicacies
while giving a finger to the past

I'll find peace whether they like me
Or not

Because if I don't like me what's the point
In giving them a peace that sacrifices my own

Death is not the end

She showed me what it meant
To never forget or take the easier path
To let death make invisible the ones
that mattered the most in life

I saw her acts of love and kindness
In her refusal to accept less than the truth
Though the pain in doing it
shone through movements and eyes
Every single time

The moments others barely saw
Deemed small by the world
Are the neon lights I learned what love
could actually look like

Regrets

You ask me if I have any regrets.

They seep in beneath my skin with time and thought
But not as many as you might think.

Regrets of my past lay few and far between
Like tumbleweeds passing slowly along
On the road of my life between them and now

The regrets of my life are the mere moments
Where I hesitated and lacked the faith and trust
Of myself, my instincts, and my own mind.

I know what you are wanting to ask
but fear to voice the words you know are offensive
So you go about it, and around it hoping I will answer
The words you dare not speak

About the big decisions you see as my pivot points in life

No, I do not regret them.

Those moments are not the big gasp you gave them
Those moments are pure bliss
They were the easy decisions where I chose
Love and trust, and found honesty in myself

They are the moments I found my first steps
In giving myself the respect and love
to use my stronger voice

Self Awareness

She praises it as though
Not everyone examines themselves
On a daily or hourly basis

Was self awareness not innate
In every living creature
That breathed and lived?

It hasn't been an easy journey
This examinations of myself twisted up in false ideas
Of 'normal' and 'right'

With fear held over me
I only ever saw the things
That were 'wrong'

Those things that would send me to hell

But this was a hell on it's own
When night came and sleep wouldn't
My brain filled with thoughts
That raced around and through my body

Intent in its determination to crash
like loud cars that stole my ability to think
Just as my fingers brushed upon an understanding
Or a truth previously laid buried

I knew there would be more nights,
Searching for my apparent self awareness
Even as false knowledge of being broken
Still held space in the very core of me

Only Kind of Perfect

He wants to climb trees and rock the doll to sleep
Roar like a dinosaur and draw the beauty.

He tells me all the stories in his head
Creates ideas and thoughts in all means available

He helps in the kitchen and with the vacuuming
He reminds me to hang out the washing
So he can help by handing me pegs

I am not perfect but for him
I am everything he needs
And that's the only kind of perfect
I ever need to be

Beautiful Tears

What makes you burst into beautiful tears?

You know that moment
When it strikes your heart
Creates warmth in your chest
And the tears prick at the back of your eyes

Is it something visual, or aural
Maybe it's the scent that wafted through the open window
or from the person who walked passed and wasn't them.

Is it the heartbreak and passion
In the musicians voice as she sings live to a crowd
Using her platform to expose her pumping heart

Is it the river flowing, winking at the sunset and slipping past her horizon

Or just the smell of freshly bitten green apples

Whatever it is
Find it
Tell it
Scream it to the world

There needs to be more beautiful tears

Rebellion

To love myself is an act of rebellion
To be proud of my own catastrophes
is a shameful act

I am shrouded in layers that weigh me down
But with each laugh and puddle jump
Another layer is sloughed away

I contradict myself constantly
And I love every breakdown, eventually

The chill keeps me alive and makes my laugh
Loud and real and unencumbered
And it reminds me to dance in the rain
Even as my teeth chatter

I will do the work to heal
And embrace the damage that needs
gentle kindness from me
And rebellion toward them

Each rainbow I see in the light and water
washes away another criticism
leaving space for my own love
to hold more worth than I had been offered

A Story of Words

I slow my words, when I can
and catch them before they're loosed again
Sliding too easily down the path
warn in to the landscape
by repetition and cruelty

The words stick in my throat as dry as days old bread
when not enough water in the world
will allow me to swallow them

so I examine the ones I've learned
to shy from and keep in dark corners

I pick them up and turn them over
only to find the sharp edges are easily smoothed

and no word is inherently good or evil
just the intent forced upon them

Still the power remains in them
when each time they slip through my lips
I flinch at the sound of my voice
landing in my ears spewing the same cruelty

It's time to change the landscape
I whisper softly beneath the gentle silence
Marking places with new tracks
made by gentle hands and softer footsteps
Made with patience and with love

I'm digging holes and replanting the trees
I'm making beautiful again those that were bent and broken
by rough hands and sharper tongues

I pluck the splinters from fingers that tremble and shake
unused to the soft lullaby of kindness

With love and a touch of dark humour
I could be kinder to myself
and change the story of these words

Acknowledgements

First and foremost I want to acknowledge the Yuggera, Jagera, and Ugarapul People who are the Traditional Owners of the country I work on and call home. I acknowledge their continued connection to land, waters and community. I pay my respects to the People, the Cultures and the Elders past, present, and emerging.

Thank you Jacinta for your gentle insistence and nudging in 2020. Without this I never would have believed my words carried poetic notes. Thank you for co-authoring our collection of poems, *Forgiving Reflections*. Several poems in *Rebellious Thoughts at Midnight* were originally published in *Forgiving Reflections*. Some have been edited, changed, and added to while others remain exactly as they once were.

There are so many people I need to thank.

Some of these incredible humans both directly and indirectly helped this collection come together. And all of them have given this often imposter-syndrome plagued author the confidence and courage to put it out there for y'all to read.

To the Annotation Rotation crew for your insane message threads that make me chuckle every morning, and the mix of sarcasm and encouragement I can always count on. To the early morning Aussie group (with special thanks to Cheyenne Blue) without your accountability of getting my bum out of bed and to the computer I'd be a lot further behind on this writing journey.

To Sarah, thank you for letting me take off the mask and dance in the rain. To Cheyenne Blue, Liz Rain, and S.R. Silcox, thank y'all for the amazing fun, laughs, and wacky adventures we have at each and every event we attend together selling each other's books (and sometimes our own) with enthusiasm and affection.

Always, to my partner and kiddo. Without you both, none of this would be possible. Thank you for everything you bring to my world. For the colours, the music, and the dancing. I can't express how much your encouragement and support have made me the author I am today.

To all of my readers who make any of this possible, thank you so much for wanting my words in your hands.

Be Safe
Be Brave
Be Kind

Neen

Also by

Novels by Neen Cohen
The Void
Coffee, Cars, and Necromancy
Children of the Gods

Novels with Adrian J Smith
Love Tails and Battle Wails Series
Book 1: Deep Sounding Chaos
Book 2: Surface Pressure
Book 3: Battle Fluke

www.ingramcontent.com/pod-product-compliance
Lightning Source LLC
Chambersburg PA
CBHW031253290426
44109CB00012B/569